RACHMANINOFF - Very Best
for piano

Sergei Rachmaninoff
(1873-1943)

Catalog #07-2032

ISBN 978-1-56922-070-2

CREATIVE CONCEPTS
P U B L I S H I N G

EXCLUSIVELY DISTRIBUTED BY

HAL•LEONARD®
CORPORATION

Visit Hal Leonard Online at
www.halleonard.com

RACHMANINOFF - Very Best
for piano

Contents

Rachmaninoff
as a pupil at the
St Petersburg
Conservatory,
early 1880s

With his
daughter Irina on
the steps of their
house at Ivanovka,
1912

With his wife, Natalya, 1922

In his New York apartment, early 1940s

PRELUDE IN C SHARP MINOR

(Opus 3. No. 2)

Sergei Rachmaninoff
(1873-1943)

(Andante)

BARCAROLLE

(Opus 10, No. 3)

Sergei Rachmaninoff
(1873-1943)

Moderato

13

Con moto

ELEGIE IN E FLAT MINOR

(Opus 3, No.1)

Sergei Rachmaninoff
(1873-1943)

Moderato

Più vivo

HUMORESQUE

(Opus 10, No. 5)

Sergei Rachmaninoff
(1873-1943)

Andante

ETUDE-TABLEAU
(Opus 33, No. 1)

Sergei Rachmaninoff
(1873-1943)

Allegro non troppo
molto marcato

ETUDE-TABLEAU

(Opus 33, No. 2)

Sergei Rachmaninoff
(1873-1943)

40

41

ETUDE-TABLEAU
(Opus 33, No. 6)

Sergei Rachmaninoff
(1873-1943)

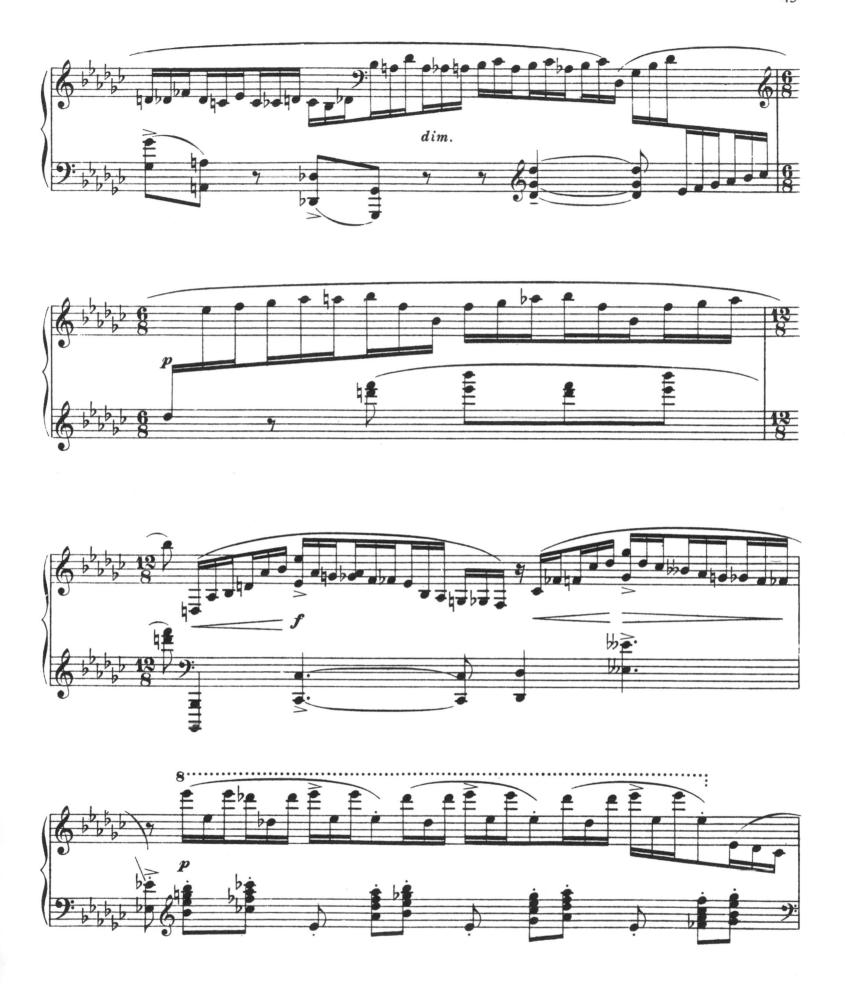

ETUDE-TABLEAU

(Opus 33, No. 7)

Sergei Rachmaninoff
(1873-1943)

ETUDE-TABLEAU
(Opus 39, No. 7)

Sergei Rachmaninoff
(1873-1943)

54

PRELUDE IN E FLAT MAJOR

(Opus 23, No. 6)

Sergei Rachmaninoff
(1873-1943)

MELODIE IN E MAJOR

(Opus 3, No. 3)

Sergei Rachmaninoff
(1873-1943)

Adagio sostenuto

PIANO CONCERTO No. 2

(Theme of Part Two)

Sergei Rachmaninoff
(1873-1943)

POLICHINELLE IN F SHARP MINOR

(Opus 3, No. 4)

Sergei Rachmaninoff
(1873-1943)

PRELUDE IN G MINOR

(Opus 23, No. 5)

Sergei Rachmaninoff
(1873-1943)

Alla marcia. (♩=108)

Un poco meno mosso.

Tempo I.

PRELUDE IN G FLAT MAJOR

(Opus 23, No. 10)

Sergei Rachmaninoff
(1873-1943)

PRELUDE IN C MAJOR

(Opus 32, No. 1)

Sergei Rachmaninoff
(1873-1943)

PRELUDE IN B FLAT MINOR

(Opus 32, No. 2)

Sergei Rachmaninoff
(1873-1943)

95

PRELUDE IN E MAJOR

(Opus 32, No. 3)

Sergei Rachmaninoff
(1873-1943)

Allegro vivace.

PRELUDE IN E MINOR

(Opus 32, No. 4)

Sergei Rachmaninoff
(1873-1943)

105

PRELUDE IN G MAJOR
(Opus 32, No. 5)

Sergei Rachmaninoff
(1873-1943)

PRELUDE IN F MINOR

(Opus 32, No. 6)

Sergei Rachmaninoff
(1873-1943)

PRELUDE IN F MAJOR

(Opus 32, No. 7)

Sergei Rachmaninoff
(1873-1943)

117

PRELUDE IN A MINOR

(Opus 32, No. 8)

Sergei Rachmaninoff
(1873-1943)

PRELUDE IN A MAJOR

(Opus 32, No. 9)

Sergei Rachmaninoff
(1873-1943)

PRELUDE IN B MINOR
(Opus 32, No. 10)

Sergei Rachmaninoff
(1873-1943)

PRELUDE IN B MAJOR

(Opus 32, No. 11)

Sergei Rachmaninoff
(1873-1943)

PRELUDE IN G SHARP MINOR
(Opus 32, No. 12)

Sergei Rachmaninoff
(1873-1943)

PRELUDE IN D FLAT MAJOR

(Opus 32, No. 13)

Sergei Rachmaninoff
(1873-1943)

141

VALSE IN A MAJOR

(Opus 10, No. 2)

Sergei Rachmaninoff
(1873-1943)

Allegro moderato

ROMANCE
(Opus 10, No. 6)

Sergei Rachmaninoff
(1873-1943)

Andantino, quasi sognando

VOCALISE

(Opus 34, No. 14)

Sergei Rachmaninoff
(1873-1943)

SERENADE

(Opus 3, No. 5)

Sergei Rachmaninoff
(1873-1943)

Tempo di Valse *(non troppo vivo)*

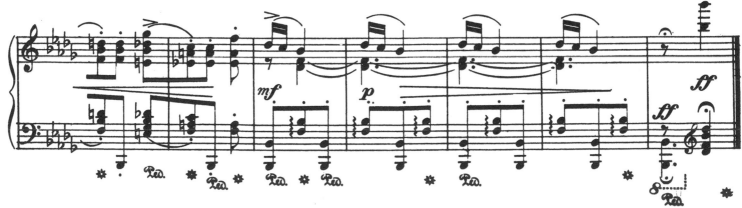